# Stripping Away
## the
# INSANITY
## of
# LIFE
## and
# PARENTHOOD!
### Volume I

## COMIC STRIP MAMA!
### aka Tanya Masse

**STRIPPING AWAY THE INSANITY OF LIFE & PARENTHOOD!**

www.comicstripmama.com

FIRST EDITION TRADE PAPERBACK

November 13, 2013

ISBN: 978-0-9936036-1-7

Cover designed by Tanya Masse and Ryan Doan.
www.ryandoan.com

DISCLAIMER

This book contains adult content and comics that are intended for entertainment and humor purposes only and should not be taken too seriously.

# Praise for Stripping Away the Insanity of Life & Parenthood

"Sister, daughter, mother-in-law, bestie, new mommy, neighbor, lady at church, grandma, postal worker, BFF, dry-cleaning lady…oh, shoot. I will just count up how many birthdays I have in a year and buy a case of these books! There's not a woman I know who wouldn't be able to relate, feel validated and LOL (a lot!) in the process!" —Jennifer Quinn, author of *Not Your Ordinary Parenting Book*

"I just finished Comic Strip Mama's new book, *Stripping Away the Insanity of Life and Parenthood.* Tanya has done it again! This book is a gem! Each page is full of hilarious, uplifting and inspirational comics as well as words of wisdom and advice for living our best life! Tanya has taken every day events and found the funny in each and every one! Once again, she uses her wonderful sense of humor and brilliant gift of writing to help us all feel better about our own circumstances! I loved this book and will recommend it to everyone I know!" —Carolyn Coppola, author of *Minivans, Meltdowns & Merlot*

"Tanya (aka Comic Strip Mama), author of the popular book *Stairway to Awesomeness* has done it again! With humor and an unrelenting positive attitude, *Stripping Away the Insanity of Life and Parenthood* both made me laugh and inspired me. Utilizing thoughtful words and clever comic strips, this book showcases Tanya's characteristic blend of sarcasm and heart." —Karen Blessing, contributing author of *The Mother of All Meltdowns*

# Dedications & Special Mentions!

This book is dedicated with ALL my love, heart and soul to:

My amazing, wonderful, awesome sons, daughter
& daughter-in-loves:

Joshua, Jamie, Lexie, Courtney & Alexis

&

My amazing, wonderful, awesome "Lover Man":

Kevin

&

All of my amazing, wonderful, awesome family, friends and
readers who have believed in me, encouraged me and
supported my journey!

&

My Angel Crystal
Special dedication in the back of book!

# Contents

# Contents

# I Have a Confession to Make...

In my LAST book, *Stairway to Awesomeness*, I told ya that my NEXT book would be ALL about "the awesome, the drama and the insanity" of PARENTHOOD!

Well guess what?!

Heh...This is my NEXT book and it is not THAT book. Only because I had an overwhelming amount of requests to publish a "best of Comic Strip Mama 2013" type novelty comic book and I do what I'm told. ;)

So my NEXT book, AFTER this book, will really be ALL about...

The AWESOME
The DRAMA
and
The INSANITY
Of PARENTHOOD!

If you didn't read my debut book, *Stairway to Awesomeness*, you can disregard this entire confession. BUT! If you haven't read it, I think you really should consider reading it.

Just sayin'. ;)

# Interview With a Stripper

**HEADLINE NEWS!**

## MOM TURNS STRIPPING HOBBY INTO SUCCESSFUL BUSINESS!

Comic Strip Mama ™

Stripping away the insanity of life and parenthood!

IF ANYONE can do it, she can!

Hot Spicy Chai

Leslee

©2012 Comic Strip Mama Enterprises Inc.

That's right folks! Tanya Masse aka: "Comic Strip Mama" is taking the world by storm with her stripping humor and inspiration!

At first, we had absolutely no clue what kind of stripping she was referring to until we got down to the bottom of it in our interview featured on Page 2...

**Q.** So, you are a stripper and you love it?

**A.** Yes! I absolutely love being a stripper!

**Q.** What do you love most about being a stripper?

**A.** I love that I put a smiles on faces every single day and that I'm making a positive difference in the world doing something that I love.

**Q.** Why do you strip?

**A.** I'm addicted to stripping. I could strip all day long.

**Q.** Did you always dream of being a stripper?

**A.** Well I don't think anyone really dreams of becoming a stripper. I didn't start stripping until my late 30's. I decided to try it and discovered I had a natural talent for stripping.

**Q.** How did you get started?

**A.** I started stripping online.

**Q.** Do you make a lot of money stripping?

**A.** Honestly, I don't strip for the money. I actually started stripping as a hobby, but then I realized that I could turn it into a business.

**Q.** So you own your own stripping business?

**A.** Yes.

**Q.** Do you employ other strippers?

**A.** No. I'm the only stripper right now.

**Q.** Are you married or single?

**A.** I am not married, but I have been blessed with an amazing man who is my life partner.

**Q.** Do you have children?

**A.** Yes. I have 3 awesome children.

**Q.** What does your family think about you being a stripper?

**A.** They love it and they support me 100%. They often watch me strip when they can and they help me come up with new stripping ideas.

**Q.** How often do you strip?

**A.** I strip every day, several times a day. When you love what you do for a living, you don't work a day in your life right?

**Q.** Who do you strip for?

**A.** I would say that I mostly I strip for other moms and women. I do have some what I call "man fans", but they aren't really my target market for my style of stripping.

**Q.** Ok, so let me get this straight... You are a female stripper that strips for other females?

**A.** Mostly. Oh and I don't only strip myself, I strip other people too. It's one of the services that I offer.

**Q.** Wow! Okay. Do you do anything else besides stripping?

**A.** Yes. I have an online novelty shop and I'm a published author.

**Q.** So you are a novelty merchant / author / stripper?

**A.** I guess you can say that.

**Q.** How many books have you published?

**A.** One so far, but I plan to publish many more.

**Q.** What is the title of your book?

**A.** Stairway to Awesomeness. I feature my strips throughout the book.

**Q.** Really?!

**A.** Yes, really.

**Q.** What exactly is your style of stripping?

**A.** I strip away the insanity of life and parenthood.

**Q.** Ok, I'm confused. How does a stripper strip away the insanity of life and parenthood?

**A.** Easily, I just strip my real life experiences and thoughts about dealing with the insanity of life and being a parent. I also inspire and encourage others to focus on the positive, recognize the blessings and find the humor in everything through my illustrations and writing.

**Q.** Ahhhh... so you are a COMIC stripper?!

**A.** Yes, of course I'm a comic stripper... What kind of stripper did you think I was talking about?!

And there you have it! Yes! I STRIP for a living (hehe) and I love it! Being a "stripper" and a writer is something I've discovered brings great joy to my own life and to the lives of others.

My real-life name is Tanya, however, I'm also known as the creator, writer, digital illustrator and *star* of Comic Strip Mama!

Ultimately, being a parent is the most rewarding and challenging role I have been blessed with in this life and I have often thought to myself that I feel like my life is nothing but a hilarious reality comic strip series! I said this out loud one day to my little Lexie and *taa daa* "Comic Strip Mama" was born!

Ever since I can remember, I have effortlessly communicated my thoughts and sentiments through writing. When I came up with the "Comic Strip Mama" concept, I found out how creative I was with the digital illustrations. Who knew?!

My comics, my blog, my literary works and my social media platforms are simply all about encouraging others to make the best of the busyness, chaos, frustrations, challenges and INSANITY of life and parenthood and STOP taking life so seriously! I inspire others to be happy, positive people and I promote the power of respect, acceptance, love, laughter and living life to the absolute fullest! I am extremely passionate about advocating for this awesome way to live!

No matter what you are faced with in this life, you have the power to determine how you react to it (as long as you have a shred of sanity left) and this is something that I have learned over time. Throughout my own challenges of life and parenthood, I have suffered many tragedies and hardships.

Most of my life I would not accept accountability for my actions or choices. It was much easier to blame the past and the tragic adversity I lived through for my negative attitude and reckless behaviour. Eventually it occurred to me that I was just making selfish excuses and I was choosing to live that way, because I could.

Over time, I learned that if I changed my attitude and my way of thinking about things I was conditioned to believe, it would change my life. So I embarked on a mission to leave the anger and the negativity behind me once and for all. No more lies, no more depression, no more taking life way too seriously, no more false expectations and no more setting myself up for failure. The only time I look back at the past now is to remember the awesome memories, to remember what I have learned from the tragic experiences, to help someone else learn from what I have lived and to see how far I have come!

I am often asked how I have managed to get through life without completely losing my mind! Well, it certainly wasn't easy and it's a LONG story, which is why I wrote my first book, *Stairway to Awesomeness*. I felt compelled to share my tragedy-to-triumph survival story with the world in an effort to prove that you can CHOOSE a life of awesomeness if you change your way of thinking about the adversity you are faced with in life. No, it's not easy, but it is possible if you follow my fundamental Steps that I have outlined in that book.

My Comic Strip Mama venture so far has turned out to be more than anything I imagined it becoming! BUT! Above all else, it has given me the opportunity to reach, entertain and inspire others and I think it just might be my calling! I never ever feel sorry for myself anymore. I always focus on the positives, the blessings and the humor...Even in the face of adversity and I encourage others to do the same!

This book is the first of the *Stripping Away the INSANITY of LIFE & PARENTHOOD* series! It is full of comics, sass, sarcasm, Comic Strip Mama humor and inspiration! I hope you enjoy it! <3

## For the LOVE of LIFE!

Ahhhh, LIFE! Isn't it awesome?! Sometimes I say that very seriously and sometimes I say that with a sarcastic tone.

When I was a KID, I couldn't wait to be a GROWN UP... But THIS is really NOT what I EXPECTED!

The truth is, life is hard and it isn't always fair. And sometimes, life is not just hard or unfair... It's downright INSANE!

Throughout your life journey, you will experience good and bad. At times you will feel like you are on a rollercoaster of exciting or terrifying ups and downs and twists and turns. You might even feel like packing up the shreds of sanity you have left and running away.

I know I sure do at times!

©2013 Comic Strip Mama Enterprises Inc.

It's okay. We all struggle and feel this way sometimes. Don't fight it too much. It doesn't mean you are a bad person. It just means you are human.

Instead of wrestling and struggling with the insanity of life or wallowing away in a sea of self-pity, do what I do...

MANAGE IT!
OWN IT!
and
EMBRACE IT!

©2013 Comic Strip Mama Enterprises Inc.

It truly is SUCH a liberating and wonderful way to live. When you learn how to manage, own and embrace your insanity, it can't control you.

Life can be awesome regardless of circumstances, IF you choose to focus on the POSITIVE, recognize the BLESSINGS and find the HUMOR in everything.

I know what you are thinking... *Easier SAID than DONE!*
Right?

Well yes, sometimes staying focused on the positive, the
blessings and the humor in every situation IS a really hard
thing to do. Especially if you are struggling and dealing with
tragic or life changing circumstances. I do struggle with it
myself at times. However, there are two ways you can deal
with any circumstance. You can make the best of it or you
can let it get the best of you.

When you make an effort to ALWAYS make the best of
everything, that's when awesomeness happens!

When you CHOOSE to focus on the POSITIVE, recognize the BLESSINGS, find the HUMOR and make the BEST of EVERYTHING... THAT'S when AWESOMENESS HAPPENS!

©2013 Comic Strip Mama Enterprises Inc.

Want to know what the magical secret is to making the best
of everything? You just do it!

You just tell yourself that no matter what happens in life, you are going to face it head on with a positive attitude. A positive attitude is powerful. It allows you to live, love, learn and laugh even when you think you are losing your beeping mind! Yes, this is easy to do when things are la ti da and wonderful. Not so easy to do when crap hits the fan and things aren't going according to your happy plan. If you feel like you need to have a good cry or vent, that's ok! Do it! Don't hold back the tears and emotions, but don't drown in them either. Also, don't say or do things that will hurt others or yourself in the process. You can't waste precious energy on that nonsense.

Sometimes reality will push you to the edge of a cliff and it will convince you to keep looking down. But you can't keep looking down. You need to keep focusing on the positive, the blessings and the humor even when it's hard. You need to stay HIGH on awesomeness, so reality cannot destroy you!

©2013 Comic Strip Mama Enterprises Inc.

How many times have you thought to yourself, *I feel like I'm going to lose my (insert possible swear word here) mind!?*

If losing your MIND burned CALORIES... I'd be a freakin' SUPER MODEL!

©2013 Comic Strip Mama Enterprises Inc.

Seriously! If losing your mind burned calories, I would be in magazines and movies and have my banging body plastered on billboards around the world! Okay. Maybe not. ;)

Unfortunately, feeling like you are going to lose your mind sometimes is a natural part of the insanity of life. It's something you should totally come to terms with, prepare for and embrace when it happens. Your only sane option to deal with the insanity of life is to learn from it and laugh about it if you can. Honestly, laughter will help you get through some of the toughest, most insane moments you are faced with. You know that saying "laughter is the best medicine"? It's true! Laughter is a powerful drug and best of all, it's free and you can overdose on it relatively safely!

You can't take everything way too seriously or eventually you will end up in a mental institution or worse...So just don't do it. Laugh when you can and encourage others to do the same.

While we are on the subject of laughter, I should warn you that when you discover awesomeness and you focus on the humor in life A LOT, it might become a little dangerous and life threatening. LOL

I'm afraid that my death will most likely be caused by me laughing out loud at the wrong place and time!

©2013 Comic Strip Mama Enterprises Inc.

While I always try to be mindful of others and their feelings, sometimes negative people do not appreciate humor or laughter in their presence. Sometimes people who are not necessarily negative just don't appreciate certain humor and are easily offended. I try really hard to be sensitive to this and avoid crossing any lines. If I notice that I have offended someone, I apologize. It's such a simple thing to do. The whole "this is me and if you don't like it or you are offended, you can suck it" attitude is not awesome, it's awful.

If you aren't sure about the type of people you are surrounded with when you are about to whip out your humor or laugh out loud, test the water before you take that plunge. You do not want to pee anyone off to the point that they want to punch you in the face or hurt you. Nobody needs to go down like that!

Part of the insanity of life is trying to keep up with EVERYTHING that needs to be done. Sometimes it feels like a never ending vicious cycle that leaves us very little time for downtime.

©2013 Comic Strip Mama Enterprises Inc.

However, making some time for some downtime is extremely important and necessary for your mental health!

If you don't do it, eventually you will find yourself burnt out and DOWN and OUT!

And if that doesn't convince you to make some time for some downtime, you will end up OUT of TIME.

YEP! That clock will always be ticking even after your time is up. So make the most of your time while you have the opportunity and don't spend all of your energy doing EVERYTHING without spending some quality downtime on yourself.

So, if you ever feel like this...

Sometimes LIFE feels like a CONTACT SPORT that I never trained for!

©2013 Comic Strip Mama Enterprises Inc.

OR like this...

I don't even have time to have the NERVOUS BREAKDOWN I DESERVE!

©2013 Comic Strip Mama Enterprises Inc.

OR like this...

Then you really NEED to make some time for this...

Now, the opposite of doing too much ALL of the time is procrastination. And let me tell you, I can go from frantically and feverishly doing everything that needs to get done to putting everything off until the last minute.

©2013 Comic Strip Mama Enterprises Inc.

Yep! I can put the "PRO" in procrastination for sure. It's not because I am lazy, although I can be at times. It's mainly because my scatterbrain gets distracted very easily by other things and ideas!

So if the comics and thoughts throughout this book seem a little scattered or out of sorts, now you know why! =)

Allow me to humor you with some of the disorders that my Mamas-In-Crime and I have discovered and documented throughout the last year...

**ADID! "Attention Deficit Idea Disorder"**

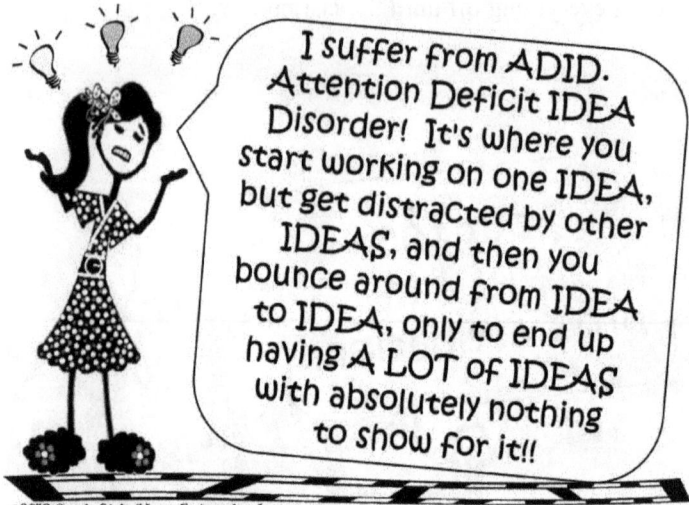

I suffer from ADID. Attention Deficit IDEA Disorder! It's where you start working on one IDEA, but get distracted by other IDEAS, and then you bounce around from IDEA to IDEA, only to end up having A LOT of IDEAS with absolutely nothing to show for it!!

©2013 Comic Strip Mama Enterprises Inc.

**ADCD! "Attention Deficit Cleaning Disorder"**

I suffer from ADCD. "Attention Deficit Cleaning Disorder." It's where you start to clean one thing, but get distracted by other things that need to be cleaned, which causes you to bounce around to different jobs only to end up doing a lot of work with nothing to show for it!!

©2013 Comic Strip Mama Enterprises Inc.

## ADOD! "Attention Deficit Organization Disorder"

I suffer from ADOD. Attention Deficit Organization Disorder! It's where you start organizing one thing, but get distracted by other things and then the phone rings, then you have to find something and then you make a mess of everything you just organized only to end up being LESS organized than you were when you started!

©2013 Comic Strip Mama Enterprises Inc.

## SD! "Sleeping Disorder"

I suffer from SD. "SLEEPING DISORDER", it's where all the voices in your head want to sleep, except for the one that wants fill your mind with random thoughts and brilliant ideas AND remember all the things you forgot to do today!

©2013 Comic Strip Mama Enterprises Inc.

Another thing I seem to struggle with as I get older is remembering stuff!

I SWEAR I spend half of my life asking myself "Why did I walk into this room?!" THEN I walk out, remember 15 minutes later, get distracted, remember again, walk back into the room and start ALL over AGAIN!

©2013 Comic Strip Mama Enterprises Inc.

Holy! Life can really wear and tear the brain to shreds it seems.

You know when you tell yourself that you MUST remember to do OR not do something and then you FORGET ?! Yeah... That's the story of my life!

Yeah.. pretty much

©2013 Comic Strip Mama Enterprises Inc.

Now let's focusing on making a living. Another aspect of life that is sometimes really hard.

©2013 Comic Strip Mama Enterprises Inc.

Seriously! Wouldn't it be wonderful if we could just be awesome all day long and get paid for it?

It would certainly make life a lot easier and less complex. There would be WAY less angry, frustrated and negative people in the world if everyone could just do what they love because they are good at it and get paid a decent living wage to do it.

Instead, the majority of people must tirelessly work their butts off for very little pay so they can struggle to make ends meet and make the big wigs rich and "successful"!

Okay, I'm going to have a little rant/vent here...I know that there are some awesome employers paying decent wages for the fruits of their labor, but there are not enough. And it makes no sense to me how anyone can think it's okay for people to make 6+ figure salaries when the faces and the foundation of their companies go home and struggle to live and provide for their families. It's sad and it sucks! But guess what?

You have to accept what you can't change and make the best of it! AND you must find the humor in it!

And if that's not the case, perhaps you have this to look forward to...

Don't think that working for yourself makes life any easier either. It really doesn't, especially in the beginning. I have experienced many emotional days when I think about wanting to give up all of the stress, planning, disciplining myself and responsibilities and just go back to working for someone else.

Bottom line... Being an entrepreneur is a risk. It's hard and it consumes a lot of your energy and time. You never know how much money you will earn from one month to the next regardless of how much you plan and forecast. Even the best of plans don't always go according to plan. I don't have benefits or a pension and at this stage of the game, most of the money I make must to go back into the business!

They say it TAKES money to MAKE MONEY... I just seem to be missing the one important aspect of this process...

©2013 Comic Strip Mama Enterprises Inc.

This is my reality. So I struggle to make ends meet too.

I know there are exception fantasy stories about successful entrepreneurs who make money effortlessly and don't have a care or worry in the world! Well, this comic strip journey is not one of them and most journeys to success aren't either.

©2013 Comic Strip Mama Enterprises Inc.

This is more like what a REAL DEAL journey to success looks like in the down-to-earth-non-fantasy-world.

So if you are struggling on your own journey to success in any aspect of your life and you feel like you are stuck in a tangled up web of confusion, making mistakes and changing your plans, don't fret! Just keep on learning and striving to achieve your goals! But don't hurt yourself or anyone else financially, mentally, physically or emotionally doing it. Some things are not worth it and if that's the case, you really need to know when to quit.

Yes, being a quitter is ok sometimes.

In closing of the "For the LOVE of LIFE" chapter of this Volume, I leave you with this last piece of scatterbrain advice...

When life gives you lemons between a rock and a hard place, look at the glass half full, grab the bull by the horns, take the road less traveled, laugh it off, be kind and just BE AWESOME!

# For the LOVE of TECHNOLOGY!

My, my, my... How things have changed. For the most part, technology is the driving force behind these changes. Some people love it, some people love to hate it, some people are addicted to it and some people absolutely despise it. Regardless of whether or not you choose to embrace technology, it will keep changing and advancing.

When you think about it, there is good and bad in everything! Even the way we lived back in the day. You should never refuse to accept something just because it's different. Most times when you give something a chance, you learn pretty quickly that it's not SO bad.

I, for one, embrace technology! I absolutely love it! It allows me to easily communicate and keep in touch with my family and friends and I really enjoy the convenience it offers. It is also the main reason I am able to entertain, inspire and reach so many people around the world! It makes me shudder when I think about how difficult all of this would have been back in the day.

Nevertheless, I still like to find the humor in the differences between "then and now".

©2013 Comic Strip Mama Enterprises Inc.

And we would totally get our little butts outside, if we knew what was good for us! ;)

©2013 Comic Strip Mama Enterprises Inc.

It's true. And yes, it's true...It was a LONG time ago!

©2013 Comic Strip Mama Enterprises Inc.

HA!

I won't say HOW, but lover man inspired this comic. ;)

I'm not going to lie. Sometimes, the internet keeps me up at night and that's not really a good thing. This is often my insanity bedtime routine...

*YAAAAWWN*

*Announce that I'm tired and I'm going to bed, if anyone is still up.

*Sign off of my social networks and close the bazillion browser tabs and software programs that I have had open all day long.

\*Close the laptop.

\*Brush my teeth, get into my jammies and get all cozy in bed.

\*Take my smartphone out of my purse and sign back into my social networks to see if anything is happening and sometimes email myself random ideas my brain decides to fill my mind with because it's not ready to shut down.

I suffer from a sleeping disorder... It's called the INTERNET!

©2013 Comic Strip Mama Enterprises Inc.

I like to think that all of this brain activity, thanks to the internet, is going to somehow benefit my brain in the long run. It should. Right?

Like anything in life, there are some really good things about technology, smartphones and the internet and there are some really bad things about it all.

I think the worst thing about it is this...

Thanks to technology, we no longer need to store certain information in our brains like we used to.

For example, back in the day I could remember numerous telephone numbers. Today, if I lost my phone, I would be up a creek!

Now, instead of storing telephone numbers, birthdays, important dates and other information in my brain, I rely on technology to store that information and feed it to me on an as-needed basis.

Now, if technology would take over some of these domestic duties, I would be one HAPPY and impressed mama!

Seriously! I think my family thinks I'm an item location specialist sometimes. Google searching for these items would make life a lot easier!

©2013 Comic Strip Mama Enterprises Inc.

Guess who wants to make a healthy well balanced meal for the entire family after a long hard day of working?! That's right! Not me!

©2013 Comic Strip Mama Enterprises Inc.

Then, we could call them "awesomephones" instead of smartphones!

Another funny thing about technology is the fact that it has pretty much reinvented the purpose of a phone.

My cell phone is a device I use for everything... EXCEPT talking to people on the PHONE!!

©2013 Comic Strip Mama Enterprises Inc.

But I think a MOM might have been the mastermind behind it!

The mastermind behind the "TEXT MESSAGE" must have been a MOM who was sick and tired of having a million different conversations while she was on the phone!

Hey MOM!

Mama?

Mommy?

©2013 Comic Strip Mama Enterprises Inc.

Now when I hear my phone ring because someone is calling me, it's always a little bit of a shock. I automatically wonder if something is wrong or if there is an emergency.

If I don't recognize the number, then I get suspicious that someone is trying to scam me or sell me something!

©2013 Comic Strip Mama Enterprises Inc.

I know what some of you are thinking. It's kinda sad that I think this way when my phone rings. However, like many, I have just gotten used to digital communication, and being a busy hard working mama, I actually really love the convenience!

So technology is what it is and yes, I do love a lot of things about it. Although I will admit that I am a little bit concerned about where technology is headed in the future.

Like anything else that evolves and changes that affects us, you either need to go with the flow or against the flow. I'm more of a go with the flow type of person. Yes it requires learning and changing, but it takes WAY more energy to go against it all. It's kinda important to keep up with the times if you don't want to wake up one morning and realize that you can't do something because you are still stuck in the stone ages!

On a lighter note, the one thing I am wholeheartedly grateful for when it comes to the internet and all this technology is the fact that I was born and raised before most of it and sometimes being older has its perks!

©2013 Comic Strip Mama Enterprises Inc.

# For the LOVE of MORNINGS & MONDAYS!

It's no secret that I am NOT a morning person.

My lover man knows it, my kiddos know it, my family knows it, my friends know it and we all understand it, joke about it and laugh about it!

It is important to be cautious around people who are not morning people. If you are not a morning person, you must tell people and warn people. It's only fair. Otherwise, you are going to end up hurting someone unintentionally one morning and that is no fun for anyone.

If you are a morning person, you have my sincere admiration! I don't know how you do it! I think morning people musta been blessed with some extra special awesome morning gene or something. Especially the people that get up early in the morning to exercise or go for a run! Wow!

I really wish I could be like that, but instead I'm like this...

©2013 Comic Strip Mama Enterprises Inc.

It's not a pretty sight, is it? It's scary. And yes, I really do look like I could audition for a KISS cover band when I first wake up in the morning.

People have told me that having children should
automatically make me a morning person...NOPE!

People have told
me that having
children should
MAKE me a
"morning person"!
OH REALLY??!!??
I don't think SO!
That's CAFFEINE!
CAFFEINE
does THAT!!

©2013 Comic Strip Mama Enterprises Inc.

The only thing that really seems to snap me out of my
morning blues is caffeine and my caffeine of choice is
coffee, which I elaborate on in the "For the LOVE of
COFFEE, CAFFEINE & TEA" chapter of this book.

The only things that are worse than mornings are MONDAY
mornings!

Every Sunday night this is me...

Guess WHO is SO excited that tomorrow is MONDAY!?!? That's right! NOT ME!

©2013 Comic Strip Mama Enterprises Inc.   services@comicstripmama.com

MONDAY

NOOOOO!! NOT YET!! GOOOOO AWAYYY!! I'm not READY!!

©2013 Comic Strip Mama Enterprises Inc.

And then every Monday morning this is me...

©2013 Comic Strip Mama Enterprises Inc.

©2013 Comic Strip Mama Enterprises Inc.

# For the LOVE of WOMANHOOD!

If you are a man reading this book, you might want to skip this chapter OR you might want to take notes. Either way, I'm not trying to relate to you, but I just might educate you!

;)

Womanhood! Isn't it awesome?!

Again, sometimes I say this sincerely and sometimes I say this with a sarcastic tone.

I love being a woman, I really do and I am grateful to be one. However, there are certain things that I love to hate about being a woman and I think most of womankind can also relate!

Women are moody.

©2013 Comic Strip 'Mama Enterprises Inc.

We really are.

But who can blame us? We start off as sweet innocent little girls...Little precious female flowers of joy. We aren't SO different in comparison to our male counterparts. The only real big difference physically is boys have a different peeing mechanism than we do. We aren't aware of all the different stuff we are made of on the inside.

Then, between the ages of 10 and 16 (and sometimes younger or older), puberty hits and we change... drastically!

We develop breasts!

We grow hair under the arms and "down under"!

We start to lay eggs, our uterus sheds and we get our lady flow for days!

We get crampy, extra sensitive, emotional and moody!

And our hormones start kicking into high gear as we embark on our journey from little girl to little woman.

From that moment on, thanks to womanhood, we struggle and suffer from a complex set of emotional and physical changes and symptoms.

Throughout the challenges of womanhood our hormones sneak up on us like ninjas! Then they RAGE and RAGE and RAGE and overload us with overwhelming and uncontrollable emotions!

They call it "PMS"... Premenstrual Syndrome. But you really can't pin point when to expect it. At least I never can.

Here is my advice about how to deal with the pesky PMS...

©2013 Comic Strip Mama Enterprises Inc.

Trust me! It's the best way to deal with PMS.

Don't mess around with it! Just give it what it wants, when it wants, how it wants and tell everyone around you to give you space and lay low until it passes.

Then, we must deal with the lady flow. Oh me oh my! We bleed for 5 to 7 days and DON'T DIE? Yessiree we do! Isn't it awesome?! No! Absolutely not.

When I see feminine product commercials on TV with happy-go-lucky energetic women wearing white who are running, exercising, dancing, swimming, riding bikes or riding horses along the freakin' beach, the only things I want to BUY are the MEDS they MUST BE ON!!

I don't know why, but I just don't feel that happy-go-lucky when I have my lady flow. I prefer to spend my lady flow days like this...

WHHHHYYYYY!!!?
WHHHHYYYY!!!??
WHY was I born
with a UTERUS
and why does it
HATE ME?!?!

©2013 Comic Strip 'Mama Enterprises Inc.

Yeah... THAT'S more like it!

Ok, that is an exaggeration. ;)

But this is not...

ANY pestering me while I'm on my lady flow will result in snarling and growling and LOUDER complaining about my cramps until I am left ALONE to whine and pig out on my junk food in peace!

©2013 Comic Strip Mama Enterprises Inc.

Okay, this might also be a slight exaggeration. But in all seriousness, the lady flow time of the month is never REALLY a happy time for anyone involved. Especially not for me and my messed up "cycles" and shedding uterus!

Actually, for some it might be a happy time, but only for that "sigh of relief" moment (if you know what I mean) and then it's emotional train wreck of cramps and bloating time again!

For those of you who are lucky enough to not have to deal with the lady flow for whatever reason, I ENVY YOU!

Then, for those of us who have babies...

Our lady parts stretch to the point that we need to put "kegel exercises" on our TO DO lists!

Our bladders never function properly ever again! Every laugh, every sneeze and every cough can result in peeing in our pants if we aren't careful!

I used to laugh and laugh and laugh when my Mama said she peed a little when she coughed or sneezed a lot... I don't laugh about that ANYMORE...

©2013 Comic Strip Mama Enterprises Inc.

After pregnancy our breasts never look the same again. EVER.

And many of us are blessed with stretch marks or "tiger stripes" as they seem to be calling them these days. I don't know about you, but my stretch marks look like Freddy Krueger left Elm Street to come and pay me a special visit! I'm sorry. I just can't glorify them. I hate them. But I do accept that I have them and of course I know how blessed I am to have 3 awesome healthy children. The end.

Some of us will also struggle with weight throughout our journey!

©2013 Comic Strip Mama Enterprises Inc.

This usually happens around the holidays!

©2013 Comic Strip Mama Enterprises Inc.

And the older you get, the harder it is to lose! The weight, that is.

Many of us just have to accept the fact that we will never be a size 0!

I'm NOT overweight, I'm just a little easier to SEE!

©2013 Comic Strip Mama Enterprises Inc.

And we need to support one another and EMBRACE IT with humor! =)

They say HEAT makes things expand. So I'm NOT overweight, I'm just HOT

©2013 Comic Strip Mama Enterprises Inc.

Then... we hit midlife. Yikes!

You mostly hear about men having a midlife crisis. Really?! Are you flippin' kidding me?!

THIS is how you know you've officially hit a midlife crisis...

You know you've officially hit a midlife crisis when the top four items on your drugstore shopping list are ACNE cream, FEMININE products, WRINKLE cream and HAIR DYE!!!

©2013 Comic Strip Mama Enterprises Inc.

I know because I'm experiencing this right now. I still get acne breakouts and I still get my lady flow, but I'm starting to get real deal wrinkles and almost every root in my head has turned to grey.

It's such a confusing time in life. My body just doesn't know what to do with itself and neither do I.

Aging is just another thing that must be embraced with a positive attitude and humor, as our hormones wind down from their long hard journey. We must also be grateful to have made it this far in life and I truly am.

But I am NOT grateful for chin hairs, out of control eyebrows or grey roots! Those suckers are annoying and embarrassing!

They are NOT "grey hairs"! They are my "WISDOM HIGHLIGHTS"!! I just happen to be extremely WISE!

©2013 Comic Strip Mama Enterprises Inc.

Then, many of us must deal with hot flashes until our hormones finally decide to be laid to rest! Our lady bodies really have to put up with a lot of insanity when you think about it!

I could tolerate HOT FLASHES a LOT better if they melted away some of my extra pounds instead of my SANITY!

©2013 Comic Strip Mama Enterprises Inc.

But, in the big scheme of things, being an awesome woman is all that really matters most in the end. <3

# For the LOVE of MEN!

MEN! I do love men. I gave birth to two of them and they are pretty awesome, if I do say so myself. I love my man children and I love my lover man with all of my heart and soul. But let's face it...Men have their ways and sometimes the things they do and say drive me completely insane!

Like over the brink! And I'm already close enough to walk!

I don't like to "bash" men and I'm not a man hater. No, no, no... I shall do none of THAT. However, I do like to find humor in all of the man vs. woman relationship stuff because like anything else in life, that's just what I do.

Every time I can find humor in something, especially difficult or frustrating experiences or situations, I WIN! And so do you! Because I turn it into comic material and I share it with you. ;)

Do you ever write "Honey Do" lists? If so, have you noticed that more often than not they end up being "Nevermind, I'll just do it myself" lists?

©2013 Comic Strip Mama Enterprises Inc.

And then, when they DO some stuff around the house, this happens...

©2013 Comic Strip Mama Enterprises Inc.

It is no secret that men really are not programmed to be very domesticated and I don't think that very many men deny this fact. I know that there are exceptions to this rule, but not really in my world.

In my little world I must give constant reminders about the fact that sometimes I feel like the maid we don't have. I must also drop little hints about how nice and awesome it would be to have a little extra help with the nitty gritty housework from time to time.

Yes, this is a little bit cruel...But hilarious! =)

Admit it ladies! Any man who helps out around the house is automatically ten times more attractive! A domesticated man makes my lady parts beep!

Forget about being oiled up and half naked... I get way more turned on by a man with a vacuum or a dishcloth in hand!

YES!

YES!

YES!

©2013 Comic Strip Mama Enterprises Inc.

In all fairness, my lover man does work very hard to provide for our family and he does do a lot of the outdoor and around-the-house maintenance stuff that I don't want any part of doing. He has also done a lot of awesome renovation work to our home.

But sometimes, this happened...

©2013 Comic Strip Mama Enterprises Inc.

And as much as I felt like I should really help out with some of the renovations to our home, I can't deny that at times, this is exactly what I was thinking.

I will admit that there are times that men do not have to be asked to help out around the house, but a lot of times when they DO help out without being asked, they make sure we know about it!

©2013 Comic Strip Mama Enterprises Inc.

One time in particular, lover man cleaned up the garage.
When he was finished, he came into the house and said,
"Guess what I just did?" Of course I asked him to tell me
what he just did. "I just cleaned the entire garage." He
responded with a big smile on his face. "That's awesome!" I
replied. But OH NO, that wasn't good enough.

"Don't you want to come and see it?" He asked extending
his hand in an effort to take mine and lead me to the garage.
So, of course, I took his hand, we walked out to the garage
and he basically gave me a grand tour of our garage and
proudly pointed out, in detail, every single little thing he
cleaned up. "Remember what that looked like before, well
look at it now." He'd say and I kept repeating, "That's
awesome!"... "That's great!"... "Wow, great job." But I'm
not going to lie, in the back of my head I kept thinking to
myself, *I don't give him a grand tour of every room in the
house when I clean them!*

Yeah, yeah...

I know there are times when men help out around the house and they just do it out of the kindness of their heart and never ask for any acknowledgement in return. It IS really awesome when they do that stuff, but it's NOT humorous comic material for this book. ;)

Sorry, I just had to poke a little more fun before I stopped talking about men and their awesome domesticationess... Yep! That would be a word from the Comic Strip Mama dictionary, not your Webster's dictionary. ;)

Now let's move on to other "for the LOVE of MEN" stuff, shall we...

They were born to nap and sleep...

AND misplace things!

They were born with selective hearing...

Men say that women talk WAY more than men... Well, that's because we have to REPEAT almost everything we say to THEM!

©2013 Comic Strip Mama Enterprises Inc.

AND selective seeing!

*sigh*

Sometimes I really do wish you could see things though my EYES, then you would notice empty toilet paper rolls!

©2013 Comic Strip Mama Enterprises Inc.

Sometimes, they are just totally oblivious...

©2013 Comic Strip Mama Enterprises Inc.

And they really don't think before they speak.

©2013 Comic Strip Mama Enterprises Inc.

Okay... Okay...

I will stop stripping about men, for now. Don't worry, I am fully aware that women also say and do things that drive men crazy and THAT is exactly what the next chapter is about!

But before I get there, I will leave you with another comic that I could not quite decide which chapter it belonged in. After struggling with this dilemma for some time, I have determined that it is a comic that kinda belongs on the cusp of these two chapters. ;)

©2013 Comic Strip Mama Enterprises Inc.

Heheh...

# For the LOVE of WOMEN!

Just as men say and do things that make women want to lose their marbles and go insane, women also say and do things that make men crazy. It's only fair for me to recognize this.

I know that most of my readership consists of women and you may be wondering why I would include such a chapter in my book. Well, when it comes to humor, I can give it and I can take it and I wholeheartedly believe that the most awesome people in the world are blessed with the ability to have a good laugh at their own expense! Remember, you can't take life too seriously.

If a woman tells a MAN he's right and no one is around to hear it, is he really right?!

Let's face it...Women are almost always the "right" one in the relationship and that is mostly because men simply LET the woman be right because they know what's good for them...Or they want to avoid having a lengthy discussion.

Men will tell you that women "nag". Yeah, sometimes we sound like we are nagging, but really, we are just reminding...

About the same things...

Several times a year or a several times a month...

Or maybe a few times a week...

And sometimes a few times a day...

©2013 Comic Strip Mama Enterprises Inc.

Okay. We nag men, but it's usually for their own good. Right?

Right! ;)

That terrifying moment when a woman asks you to guess what day it is or how much she weighs now, and you feel like you are guessing which wire to cut to diffuse a ticking BOMB!

©2013 Comic Strip Mama Enterprises Inc.

ALL women know that when we ask men questions such as these, they sweat and squirm and we love it. Even when men think they know the answer, they usually second guess themselves. Often, they will attempt to change the subject or answer our question with another question in order to buy some time and make sure they get it right. Sometimes they even pretend they didn't hear us as they casually head for the nearest exit.

All women know that we sometimes ask these types of questions just to watch men sweat and squirm.

I'll be the first to admit that I've done it to many men in my life and it is hilarious almost every time!

Men absolutely HATE this about women!

All men wish that women would just say what they mean and mean what they say...

©2013 Comic Strip Mama Enterprises Inc.

But sometimes when we are "emotional" (that's my excuse) we just don't and so we do this insanity instead...

©2013 Comic Strip Mama Enterprises Inc.

Some days we are a little cranky in the morning...

And some days we are cranky all day...

But, in all fairness most of our emotional rollercoaster shenanigans are caused by our hormone imbalance and "PMS"..."Premenstrual Syndrome"...Which, in reality, should actually be called "Pre ANYTIME OF THE MONTH Syndrome". Because in all honesty, our hormones are bouncing all over the place pretty much all month long, not just pre-menstruation!

And the fact that our menstruation is called a "period" is also a huge understatement too...

©2013 Comic Strip Mama Enterprises Inc.

Yep! That IS more like it!

This is a funny story that lover man insisted I include in this book...

One day this summer, lover man and I went shopping for some stuff. Whenever we go out shopping I'm always on lover man about saying his please and thank you's. Actually, I'm always on anyone I'm with about using manners, but this particular day it happened to be him.

So anyway, we finish shopping, the checkout clerk scans all of our purchases, lover man pays and then the clerk hands him the receipt. Instead of saying thank you, he took the receipt and stared at it as he slowly started to walk away.

So I gave him the "BIG EYES", looked at the checkout clerk and said, "thank you very much."

After a few seconds, lover man informed me that he didn't say thank you because he suspected that the clerk double charged him for an item and it turned out she did. No big deal, it was a mistake and we got it straightened out immediately.

When we got home that evening, we talked about the incident. Lover man didn't think he should have to say thank you in that circumstance and I told him that people are not perfect, they make mistakes and he should always say thank you when someone gives him something.

This was the end result of that conversation...

For the LOVE of BFFs!

Life is all about finding the special ones who are YOUR kinda CRAZY!

Life just wouldn't be as awesome without the BFF's (BEST FRIENDS FOREVER) that we find and treasure throughout the challenges of it.

They are what I like to call, "special ones".

BFF's really are SO special and important. They are an essential key element of our core life support system.

Quite often, our closest friends mean more to us and are closer to us than some of our blood family members.

BFF's are the family we hand pick for ourselves!

BFF'S are the FAMILY we pick out for ourselves!

©2013 Comic Strip Mama Enterprises Inc.

They are the people we can let loose with and laugh with.

©2013 Comic Strip Mama Enterprises Inc.

They are the people who keep us calm and comfortably insane.

©2013 Comic Strip Mama Enterprises Inc.

They understand every word we DON'T say.

©2013 Comic Strip Mama Enterprises Inc.

They do things that count, but don't count the things they do...

©2013 Comic Strip Mama Enterprises Inc.

But most importantly BFF's have a mutual understanding about this...

An AWESOME friendship does not mean that you are INSEPARABLE, It means that you CAN be SEPARATED and NOTHING CHANGES!

©2013 Comic Strip Mama Enterprises Inc.

## For the LOVE of PARENTHOOD!

Life is challenging and sometimes it's not just challenging, it's downright INSANE! When you choose to be a parent in this life, you enter a completely different zone of challenges and insanity!

It's like the twilight zone!

Can you hear the music? Ha! I can!

Because I will be publishing an entire book that will be ALL about the awesome, the drama and the insanity of parenthood, I will just touch on some basic expectations of parenthood in this book.

First off, I think it's important to acknowledge that no matter how you "conceive" a child, if you are raising a child in a loving and nurturing environment, you are considered a parent in my books.

BLOOD
doesn't make
you a
PARENT!
L♥VE DOES!

©2013 Comic Strip Mama Enterprises Inc.

Parenthood is a life long journey of living, loving, laughing and learning while losing your mind! I'm not going to sugar coat anything about it!

SANITY

PARENTHOOD!
A life long journey
of bracing yourself
for the WORST,
hoping for the
BEST and hanging
on to your LAST
shred of SANITY
for dear life!

©2013 Comic Strip Mama Enterprises Inc.

Yes, being a parent IS, or should be, the most rewarding role you will ever be blessed with in this life. But there will be times that you feel like you are being whipped to the brink of insanity and back like a YO YO!

You will shed blood, sweat and tears and you will CLEAN lots of blood, sweat, tears and some other not so nice bodily fluids and excretions along the way.

There will be mini heart attacks, ER visits, accidents, chaos and you will face your worst fears. But the overwhelming love, laughter and awesome times you experience gets you through the years!

Parenthood is a 24 hour / 7 day a week commitment! Even when your child is away from you, they never leave your mind or your heart.

PARENTS are the only people on the planet that know the TRUE meaning of 24/7!

©2013 Comic Strip Mama Enterprises Inc.

When a child NEEDS a parent, they NEED a parent. They don't care what time of the day it is or where you happen to be or what you happen to be busy doing.

Bottom line...When a child NEEDS you, they NEED you and they will FIND YOU!!

I have been a parent for almost 22 years and I have experienced it all from the womb to the empty nest. I am incredibly grateful for EVERYTHING I have blessed with throughout my journey. But the one thing I don't think I could ever live without is my sense of humor!

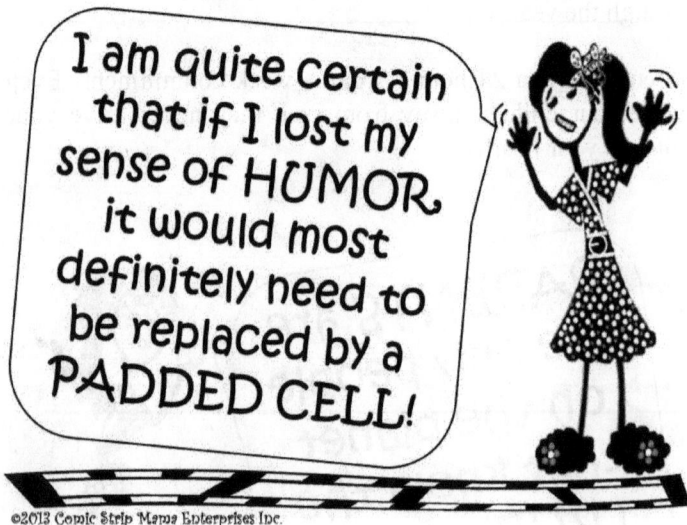

I am quite certain that if I lost my sense of HUMOR, it would most definitely need to be replaced by a PADDED CELL!

©2013 Comic Strip Mama Enterprises Inc.

I rely on my sense of humor to get me through the toughest moments of parenthood and finding the humor in it all will be the main focus of this entire chapter!

Allow me to briefly walk you through a few of the universal insanities of being a parent...

Parenthood wears you out and wears you down emotionally, mentally and physically!

The main thing we miss is SLEEP!

Babies are notorious for being nocturnal little blessings, but don't think that the sleeplessness ends when they finally start sleeping through the night. OH NO. It does not!

Yes, it does get better as our babes get older, but the cold hard truth is, once we become parents, we will never sleep the same as we did before children.

EVER.

©2013 Comic Strip Mama Enterprises Inc.

Even once our children reach the teen years and even the adult years for that matter, we continue to experience countless sleepless nights for a variety of reasons that I will elaborate on in my parenthood book. ;)

Parents also miss sitting down and relaxing for longer than a few minutes at a time.

WAAAAAA!

MOM!?
MOMMY!?
MAMA?!
MA!?

I'm pretty sure that when you sit down to relax for a moment, a silent alarm goes off alerting the KIDS that they suddenly NEED your ATTENTION!

©2013 Comic Strip Mama Enterprises Inc.

Effortlessly keeping the house clean and organized becomes a thing of the past. (Moms suffer from this the most.)

Once upon a time, I used to be able to keep my house spotless and organized... Then I had children! The END!

©2013 Comic Strip Mama Enterprises Inc.

Before you become a parent, you dream of doing it ALL and being the BEST, most perfect superstar parent on the face of the planet.

You turn your nose up at other parents that you see struggling with temper tantrums and kids that don't want to do what they're told.

You roll your eyes when you hear other parents say stuff like, "my baby NEVER sleeps!" or "I NEVER have time for myself!" or "sometimes I feel like I want to run far, far, away!" or "I feel like I'm going to lose my ever loving mind!" and you think to yourself, THAT will NEVER be ME.

Then, after you become a parent, all you want to do is PEE ALONE and then flush those pre-parent dreams down the toilet and enjoy a half a moment of silence!

©2013 Comic Strip Mama Enterprises Inc.

And eat a meal while it's still HOT!

©2013 Comic Strip Mama Enterprises Inc.

And get the laundry from the washer to the dryer all in the same day...

©2013 Comic Strip Mama Enterprises Inc.

And relax in the bath or shower...

©2013 Comic Strip Mama Enterprises Inc.

And get through an entire day without having to repeat yourself 156,654,654,697,486,849,852 times!

©2013 Comic Strip Mama Enterprises Inc.

Despite all of the challenges and insanity, being a parent is awesome for the most part. It really is. And eventually, you will get payback.

When my kids move out, I'm going to go over to their house, take off my shoes and leave them right in front of the door, turn on ALL of the lights and electronics, make a huge mess, open and close the fridge door 27 times, whine and whine that there's nothing to EAT or DO and then tell them I'm BORED and leave!

©2013 Comic Strip Mama Enterprises Inc.

Especially if your kids have kids of their own...

©2013 Comic Strip Mama Enterprises Inc.

I have only touched the surface of the awesome, the drama and the insanity of parenthood. However, I promise you that my book dedicated to parenthood will get right down to the nitty gritty about what you might REALLY expect from the womb to the empty nest!

But for now, I leave you with this final thought...

©2013 Comic Strip Mama Enterprises Inc.

Coincidence?! I think NOT! ;)

# Outta the LIPS of LIL' BLESSINGS

Throughout the challenges of our parenting years the lil blessings will say and do things that either make us proud, make us want to crawl under a rock or make us laugh out loud! Sometimes an "outta the lips of lil' blessings" moment will make you do all three all at the same time. You just never know what the lil' blessings will do or say from one moment to the next and sometimes these moments make for some of the most memorable stories that we love to share over and over again.

I asked my readers to share some of their precious "out of the lips of lil' blessings" moments with me and I selected a few for this book. My next book, about parenthood, will have a much larger "outta the lips of lil' blessings" chapter and it will include many of stories about my own lil' blessings. For this book, I will share stories from others. However, I do have one story from when I was a lil' blessing that I will share with you first.

This incident happened shortly after my dad met my stepmom so I was around 9 years old. We were enjoying a big family dinner and my father happily said, "Isn't this nice? Isn't it so nice to enjoy a nice family dinner with everyone?" And so I happily replied, "YES! It's so nice! It's like a big GANG BANG!"

Well suddenly the smile on my father's face was replaced with a look of horror and he very sternly looked at me and said, "You DO NOT say that Tanya! You never ever say that again!" I remember very quietly asking, "But why?" and he just responded, "Just don't say it again okay?!"

LOL!

I knew I said something very inappropriate because of the way my father reacted, but I never knew just HOW inappropriate it actually was until I was older and I learned exactly what a "gang bang" meant. I just thought it meant a bunch of people getting together and having a good time.

Here are a few more stories from my readers....

©2013 Comic Strip Mama Enterprises Inc.

When my son was about five, he saw a box of panty liners in the bottom of the bathroom cabinet and he asked me, "what are those really big band-aids for?!"

Natalie B.

My grandson, Nathan, caught me right after I had taken a shower. When he knocked on my bedroom door, I just grabbed a robe and held it up to cover my front. I should have known something was amiss because as he spoke to me, his eyes were just dancing. When he was finished, as I turned to close the door and get dressed, he said, "Gramma, I can see your butt!" Indeed he could, in the full length mirror that was directly behind me!

Greta Frigault

While sitting in a Tim Hortons drive-through, my hubby asks our 3 year old "vegetarian" daughter if she would like anything. Her reply was "apple juice and tomatoes please!!!!" My husband looked at me as I busted a gut in laughter and then responded "they don't sell tomatoes at Tim Hortons Sienna" her response was "ahhhhhh not fair!!!"

The Tropeano Family

I was pushing my 4 yr old daughter on the swings at a popular park and I felt my wedding ring go flying off. I was sad and it kind of surprised me that I felt upset because I don't attach much value to stuff... We looked and looked for it and then my daughter, tired of looking, said "Mom, it's just a THING ... can you push me on the swing again?"

L. Fisher

I go to the hospital to check in for my ultrasound. While waiting on the clerk in administration to take my info and get me set up she asked me, "Mrs. Marler, do you have a primary physician?" Before I could open my mouth and respond, my 4 year old son Ayden replies, "Yeah, my daddy!" All I could do was turn red in the face and the clerk could not stop laughing.

Christina Marler Kaltsas

My oldest is 26. When she was little we lived in a very small town. I went to high school there so I knew many of the people. Whenever we'd be out running errands, lots of people would honk and wave at us. One day when she was about 4 years old, we were sitting at a stop light with cars on either side. She kept asking "Who's that mommy?" I told her I didn't know. She asked a few more times and in exasperation I said, "I told you I DONT know!" She crossed her little arms and very sternly said, "You're not telling me mean mommy!!" Of course I started laughing. She didn't understand why I was laughing and started to look like she was going to cry. Just then, the light changed and someone I knew drove by and honked. I told her who it was and she said, in her sternest little girl voice, "Well, why didn't you just say so!!"

Deb M

At the time I was a mommy to an 8 year old, a 6 year old, 3 year old triplets and a 2 year old. (5 boys and 1 princess.) We were home on a Saturday afternoon and it was a "let's clean the upstairs" kind of day. I was busy with switching clothes from winter to summer and I had the kids help with cleaning under the beds, dusting and organizing the closets again. I was grateful for my two older boys, they were very helpful while the other four children were being occupied with Disney movies on the television...I know, the babysitter that I swore I would never use!

I believed we were finally done so I told the older boys to take a break while I vacuumed the bedrooms. I was thinking to myself, *I should turn on the air conditioning it's getting hot up here.* I finished with 3 bedrooms and I only had one more to go. As I was about to begin vacuuming the last bedroom, my youngest child came to me with a cup of water. He said, "drink mommy." I smiled as big as I could and my heart melted as I thought, *how sweet is he*! I accepted his gift of water and took a drink. It was refreshing so I took several gulps. Then I realized it was really cold water. I looked at my precious baby and asked him, "Dewey, where did you get this water?" He did not reply.

So, I asked the older boys if they went downstairs and gave their baby brother a cup of cold water to give to me. They shook their heads no.

I was beginning to panic and asked Dewey to show Mommy where he got the water. I took his hand and encouraged him to please take me where he got the water. He led me to the bathroom and pointed to the toilet! I gasped and said, "Dewey, did you get the water from the toilet?!" He took the cup and sure enough he dipped it in the water and offered me another refreshing cup of cold water. I praise God that at least the children remembered to flush before Dewey decided to quench his mummy's thirst.

Lori Cherry

When my daughter Kailie was about 1 and learning to talk she would refer to flowers as "wubbzies". One day my husband was in the front yard with her when Kailie picked a flower and called it a wubbzy. My husband picks another flower holds it out to her and says F-L-O-W-E-R really slowly. Kailie picks a flower holds it in front of my husband's face and said, W-U-B-B-Z-I-E really slow and deliberate! The look on my husband's face was priceless!

Rachel Lock-Weiler

# For the LOVE of SASS 'n CHEEK & SARCASM!

Although there is already a lot of sass 'n cheek and sarcasm throughout most of this book, this is a little bonus chapter for some MORE random scatterbrained sass 'n cheek and sarcasm...and of course, HUMOR!

That awkward moment when you have perfected your sarcasm skills to the point that you don't even know if you're being serious or not...

I've perfected my SARCASM skills to the point that sometimes I'M not even sure if I'm being serious or not...

It happens! Just ask Dollie Mama! ;)

SOMETIMES... my AGE is very inappropriate for my BEHAVIOR!!

Ummm..... Sometimes??!

©2013 Comic Strip Mama Enterprises Inc.

Ok, the cat's got a point!

But seriously, it's good for your mind, heart and soul to forget all about your age every once in a while and just be silly for a change.

Do you know what I LOVE about people with BAD ATTITUDES?? The fact that I am NOTHING like THEM!!

©2013 Comic Strip Mama Enterprises Inc.

F.Y.I., a bad attitude sucks and you can't blame it on anyone else except for yourself. No matter what is going on in your life, YOU are ultimately in control of YOUR attitude, your reactions and how you treat others.

Remember, it takes just as much energy to have a negative, bad attitude as it does to have a positive, awesome attitude. ;)

I'm highly allergic to NEGATIVE & DRAMA... They make me break out in HUMOR & SARCASM!

©2013 Comic Strip Mama Enterprises Inc.

If there is one thing that I am sarcastically passionate about, it's NEGATIVITY and DRAMA.

And after I break out in humor and sarcasm, I will give it right back! Life is much too short to entertain it.

I'm always leaving my jacket around and can never find it when I desperately NEED a hug!

©2013 Comic Strip Mama Enterprises Inc.

If you don't love a good challenge, think twice about becoming a parent! Chances are if you are reading this book... it's too late for you too. I don't remember being taught this in school. Sex education classes in school should really involve real life children whining and asking question after question for hours at a time.

©2013 Comic Strip Mama Enterprises Inc.

It's kinda funny how as you get older, you start enjoying the things you hated as a kid such as nap time, time-outs and letting other people do stuff for you.

©2013 Comic Strip Mama Enterprises Inc.

You know that awesome feeling when you want to figure out what to make and then slave over a hot stove after a long hard day? Yeah! Me neither!

©2013 Comic Strip Mama Enterprises Inc.

And when I ask my family what they want for dinner, the answer is usually "I don't care" or "I don't know" or "whatever"! I think I wouldn't mind cooking so much if I had a little help.

My doctor asked me if I have ever had a "STRESS TEST" and I said, "Of COURSE! I'm a PARENT! My KIDS give me a STRESS TEST sometimes SEVERAL times in one DAY!

©2013 Comic Strip Mama Enterprises Inc.

Medical stress tests should involve children whining and crying and asking question after question while you are trying to concentrate on doing multiple tasks. THAT would be way more realistic than walking on a treadmill.

©2013 Comic Strip Mama Enterprises Inc.

Sanity is so tricky sometimes!

©2013 Comic Strip Mama Enterprises Inc.

It's a vicious cycle that totally gets worse with age.

Sometimes my brain is like the BERMUDA TRIANGLE, thoughts fly IN and are never to be found again!

There will be a documentary about this on the discovery channel... If I can remember... what was I just saying?

Sometimes, when I ask someone in my house to do something, I've realized that I'm actually just telling MYSELF what to do out LOUD!

I tell myself what to do out loud pretty much every single day.

LOL! I just love this comic. It's a popular t-shirt comic too!

Bahahahahaha! Get it?

©2013 Comic Strip Mama Enterprises Inc.

Don't you love how you can now buy Halloween, Thanksgiving and Christmas stuff at the end of August?!

Soon they will just have it out all year!

©2013 Comic Strip Mama Enterprises Inc.

Sarcasm is my self-defense of choice!

©2013 Comic Strip Mama Enterprises Inc.

These days,
"getting lucky"
means walking
into a room and
remembering
WHY!

©2013 Comic Strip Mama Enterprises Inc.

Keep
CALM...
SMILE...
And let
KARMA
deal with it.

©2013 Comic Strip Mama Enterprises Inc.

Whenever I'm overwhelmed with the mess in my house I just lie on the couch and stare at the ceiling... The ceiling is clean...

Is It WINO'Clock Yet??

©2013 Comic Strip Mama Enterprises Inc.

You know that awesome feeling when you go to bed, fall asleep immediately, stay asleep all night and then wake up feeling rested and refreshed?! Yeah...Me neither!

©2013 Comic Strip Mama Enterprises Inc.

©2013 Comic Strip Mama Enterprises Inc.

# For the LOVE of COFFEE, CAFFEINE & TEA!

It's no secret that I love, love, LOVE coffee! But I'm not addicted...

No, no...I'm just in a committed relationship with its warm deliciousness that wakes me up, touches my soul and replenishes a few shreds of morning sanity.

That's all...

I am NOT addicted to COFFEE... WE are just in a committed relationship!

But coffee is good for you and it increases your life expectancy! I heard it on the news and read it on the internet, so it must be true!

Here are a slew of the most popular Comic Strip Mama coffee, caffeine and tea comics that I have posted over the last year. I hope you enjoy them.

©2013 Comic Strip Mama Enterprises Inc.

Sometimes it is absolutely necessary to sneak around your own house like a cat burglar so you can actually drink an entire cup of coffee while it's still HOT!

Sometimes...It's mission impossible.

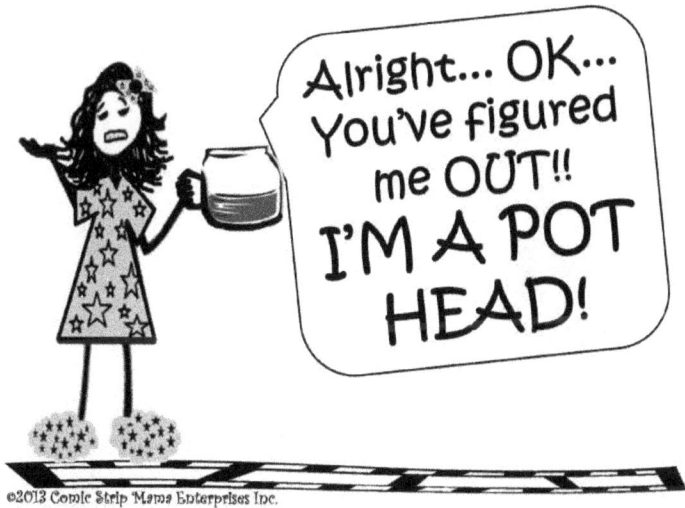

A COFFEE "pot head" of course!

If I could learn how to play guitar, I would definitely start strumming up coffee songs and posting videos on You Tube.

OF COURSE I love YOU more than COFFEE, but PLEASE don't make me PROVE IT!

©2013 Comic Strip Mama Enterprises Inc.

Our relationship would be in jeopardy if he made me prove it! Yikes!

I can't even imagine what would happen if my lover man all of a sudden gave me an "It's me or the coffee!" ultimatum.

Pffft! Like that would ever happen... he would never be that cruel.

Before I've had my COFFEE, I am whatever the opposite of "BRIGHT EYED and BUSHY TAILED" is!!

Where did that saying "bright eyed and bushy tailed" even come from?! If we are going to compare humans to animals first thing in the morning, then I would have to say that before I've had my morning coffee fix, I'm more like a wild and starving animal with rabies.

Here's a list of things I'd be HAPPY to do before I've had my first cup of COFFEE!!

The hardest part of being an "I need coffee" person is making it when you haven't had any. I barely have enough energy to stir my coffee before I've had a sip of coffee in the morning.

©2013 Comic Strip Mama Enterprises Inc.

Sometimes I write "drink coffee" on my TO DO list so I know I will definitely accomplish something on the list that day.

Ummm, oopsie daisy! But coffee is GOOD for you! Right?!

Yes. Size DOES matter! The BIGGER the BETTER!

©2013 Comic Strip Mama Enterprises Inc.

Betcha thought I was changing my mind about being a morning person... NOPE!

©2013 Comic Strip Mama Enterprises Inc.

This is how I feel right now at this very moment! It's almost 10:30 pm and I'm still WORKING! SO many things to do, so little time!

©2013 Comic Strip Mama Enterprises Inc.

WebMD doesn't have this disorder listed yet, but it should be. It should be taken very seriously!

©2013 Comic Strip Mama Enterprises Inc.

I am definitely a MOMBIE! There should be a MOMBIE reality TV series or movie. I could totally star in it!

©2013 Comic Strip Mama Enterprises Inc.

A TEA "pot head", of course!

©2013 Comic Strip Mama Enterprises Inc.

I take this survey every day and I end up with the same results.

©2013 Comic Strip Mama Enterprises Inc.

My "PEOPLE" being my fellow coffee lovers! Coffee lovers unite!

©2013 Comic Strip Mama Enterprises Inc.

You betcha! Very little would get done without it!

That is why I call them both my "liquid sanity".

This is another one of those cusp comics. It belongs in this chapter, but it equally belongs in the next!

# For the LOVE of WINE & BEVERAGES of the ADULT KIND!

Now, let me make a little disclaimer before we go further...

Yes, I strip about drinking wine and beverages of the adult kind. BUT I, like millions of other adults in the world, consume and enjoy alcohol legally, reasonably and responsibly. All of my alcohol related comics are intended for adult entertainment and humor purposes only. Period. ;)

Also, it is NEVER okay to drink and drive.

I don't mean to get all technical, but according to chemistry ALCOHOL is a SOLUTION!!

It's true...Just stating a scientific fact.

©2013 Comic Strip Mama Enterprises Inc.

This wine comic is my pride and joy! It's one of the first ones I came up with that went viral!

If you can't fix it with duct tape or wine, it ain't worth fixin'!

LOL

©2013 Comic Strip Mama Enterprises Inc.

Wine is good for you and it increases your life expectancy. Again, I heard this on the news and read it on the internet so it's true!

©2013 Comic Strip Mama Enterprises Inc.

Seriously, whining CAN cause WINING! And that's a fact!

Bahahah! As if I would ever do this...But it would be hilarious!

Think about how many bottles of wine the price of a diamond can buy!

©2013 Comic Strip Mama Enterprises Inc.

LOL!

©2013 Comic Strip Mama Enterprises Inc.

Bahahaha! Admit it, this is hilarious and perfect.

©2013 Comic Strip Mama Enterprises Inc.

Some hilarious nonsense for my beer lovers!

©2013 Comic Strip Mama Enterprises Inc.

I'm easy!

Shhhhhhhhhh... Don't tell lover man! ;)

©2013 Comic Strip Mama Enterprises Inc.

Heheh...

©2013 Comic Strip Mama Enterprises Inc.

Sometimes the best thing to do is screw it, pour it, put your feet up and sip the wine down!

©2013 Comic Strip Mama Enterprises Inc.

You know it's been a long hard week when...

©2013 Comic Strip Mama Enterprises Inc.

Yes it does!

©2013 Comic Strip Mama Enterprises Inc.

Sometimes it's the best thing to do!

©2013 Comic Strip Mama Enterprises Inc.

Yes please!

©2013 Comic Strip Mama Enterprises Inc.

I stripped this as a special request for some awesome ladies who were stuck in an emergency shelter because their homes were flooded. They wanted me to come up with something to make them laugh. They requested a comic about needing wine in their situation. This is what I came up with! ;)

©2013 Comic Strip Mama Enterprises Inc.

If I ever had to meditate, I would have to drink wine to relax my brain enough to meditate. So I just kill two birds with one stone.

©2013 Comic Strip Mama Enterprises Inc.

I have a confession to make. Not one pair of my yoga pants have been to yoga.

# The BEST of the "Mamas-In-Crime!"

In my last book, I briefly introduced you to some of my awesome Mamas-In-Crime. In this book, I would like to give them a little more time in the spotlight because they absolutely deserve it!

For those of you who don't know, each one of the main mama characters in my comic strip are based on real deal people that I know and love. Some strips that feature them may not necessarily be based on their actual real life per se, however, lots of the comic materials I strip are based on the ideas they come up with.

Each one of these fine ladies has contributed to my comic journey in their own special way. Not only have they fed me oodles and oodles of awesome comic material, they have supported me, inspired me, believed in me and encouraged me every step of the way!

Mamasita

Gramma

Dollie Mama

Maggie Wise Mama

Cheryl Mama

Creelmama

Red Hot Mama

This entire chapter will feature all of my main Mamas-In-Crime! I hope you enjoy!

©2013 Comic Strip Mama Enterprises Inc.

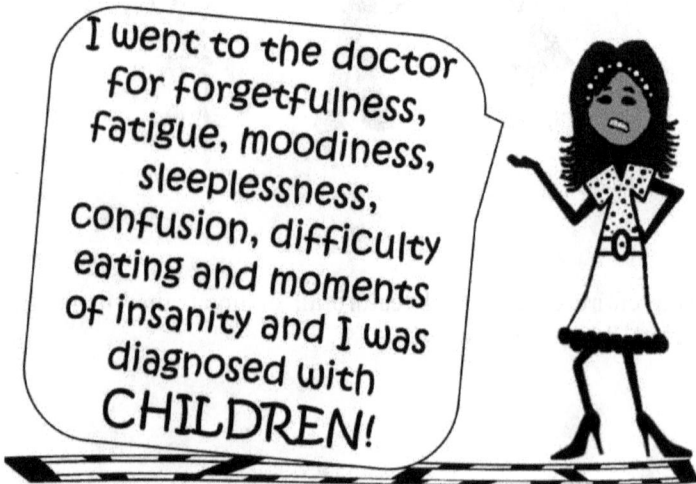

©2013 Comic Strip Mama Enterprises Inc.

I think this is a universal song of all the mamas of the world!

©2013 Comic Strip Mama Enterprises Inc.

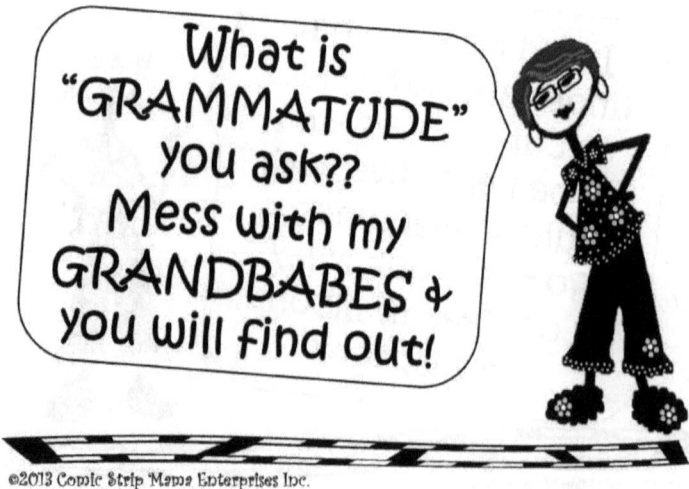

©2013 Comic Strip Mama Enterprises Inc.

©2013 Comic Strip Mama Enterprises Inc.

©2013 Comic Strip Mama Enterprises Inc.

©2013 Comic Strip Mama Enterprises Inc.

©2013 Comic Strip Mama Enterprises Inc.

©2013 Comic Strip Mama Enterprises Inc.

©2013 Comic Strip Mama Enterprises Inc.

©2013 Comic Strip Mama Enterprises Inc.

©2013 Comic Strip Mama Enterprises Inc.

©2013 Comic Strip Mama Enterprises Inc.

©2013 Comic Strip Mama Enterprises Inc.

Are you EVER coming to BED?

When I said I would go to bed right after I was finished the chapter, I meant the LAST chapter!

www.cherylktardif.com

©2013 Comic Strip Mama Enterprises Inc.

You know you're a WRITER when... YOU see someone holding a SHOVEL while standing in their backyard, and you're wondering where they buried the BODY!!"

www.cherylktardif.com

©2013 Comic Strip Mama Enterprises Inc.

©2013 Comic Strip Mama Enterprises Inc.

©2013 Comic Strip Mama Enterprises Inc.

They say the smarter a woman is, the harder it is for her to find the right man... I must be a GENIUS!

I just changed my relationship status to... "Ain't nobody got time for THAT!"

©2013 Comic Strip Mama Enterprises Inc.

# Comic Strip Mama Inspirational Quotes

There will be HIGHS & LOWS
There will be CHALLENGES
There will be INSANITY
There will be OBSTACLES
There will be MISTAKES
There will be FAILURES
There will be LESSONS
There will be DOUBTERS
BUT if you choose to focus on the
POSITIVE, recognize the
BLESSINGS & find the
HUMOR in it ALL...
There will be AWESOMENESS!

~ Comic Strip Mama 31/07/13

comicstripmama.com    ©2013 Comic Strip Mama Enterprises Inc.

"When you focus on the POSITIVE, the BLESSINGS and the HUMOR and just do your thing and you stop worrying SO much about what every one else is thinking and doing and STOP taking life WAY too seriously... AWESOMENESS happens!"

~ Comic Strip Mama 12/07/13

"Quit struggling to be "normal"... It doesn't exist. Just be YOUnique & AWESOME!"

~ Comic Strip Mama 10/07/13

"If there ever comes a time that you forget where you came from, you've gone too far!"

~ Comic Strip Mama 27/07/13

"If you CAN help someone, DO IT! The WORLD needs more of THAT!"

~ Comic Strip Mama 17/08/13

©AntiBULLYotics

"If you CAN make someone LAUGH who has every reason to cry, DO IT! The WORLD needs more of THAT!"

~ Comic Strip Mama 18/08/13

© AntiBULLYotics

"People cannot live forever, but memories can. Never pass up an opportunity to create awesome memories with your special ones."

~ Comic Strip Mama 25/08/13

"If you are surprised by the things I say and do, then you really haven't paid attention to who I am."

~ Comic Strip Mama 28/09/13

comicstripmama.com

Your opinion should always be based on what you have seen with your own eyes, what you have heard with your own ears and what you have felt with your own heart.

07/08/13

"Two things define you...
your attitude when
you have nothing and
your attitude when
you have everything."

The things you
should value most
in this life are
NOT things.

## My Very Special Dedication to
## My Angel CRYSTAL

Have you ever walked into a wall, a door, a window, a pole or even a PERSON because you were off in la la land and you weren't really paying attention?

I have physically walked into many of these things more than once throughout the challenges of my life! One time, I walked into a corner of a wall at WORK... in front of clients! I laughed it off, and so did the clients and my co-workers, but I almost split the middle of my forehead open and ended up with a nice sized goose egg and a headache to go with it.

Another time I walked into a cement pillar. Another time I walked into a stop sign pole. Oh and another time I ran full force into a person (I was running, watching my feet), knocked myself out and landed flat on my back.

These mentions are only a few incidents. There have been many. I guess you can say this is how I go through life sometimes... I get busy and I keep going and doing everything without REALLY taking time to pay better attention to my surroundings and then BAM... The powers that be teach me a little lesson... "STOP, SLOW DOWN, LOOK AROUND YOU and PAY ATTENTION!"

These incidents do not only happen physically. They happen figuratively too. When life throws you a curveball or hits you with another blow that affects you emotionally and mentally.

This year has been an awesome one and I am so grateful for that! However, I have spent A LOT of time turning my comic hobby into a business and writing my books and that has been no small feat. It's been exhausting, challenging and rewarding all at the same time. I'm doing what I love and I'm living my dream. But like I said, it has consumed a lot of my time. Although I realize that all of this preliminary hard work is a necessary evil of being an entrepreneur and a new author, the last few months have taught me that I missed out on some precious moments with my family and friends. I have taken some things for granted. The number one thing being TIME.

Throughout the challenges of this year I have quite often not spent enough time with my special ones because I have been SO BUSY! I have managed to successfully balance almost everything... when it comes to my kids. But many other special people in my life have been pushed aside.

"Next year will be different, I will have more time." This is what I have been telling myself and others.

Well, on the evening of August 25$^{th}$ I received a text from my son:

"Mom? Did you hear about Crystal?"

Crystal is a very good friend of mine and that morning, she passed away. Wow! She was only 34! I couldn't believe it and it's still hard to believe. All I know is that she fought a very short and hard battle with lung, liver and bone cancer. WTH!? I didn't even know she was sick! The first thing I thought was, WHY didn't she tell me?! I would have taken time to go see her. But talking to another friend of hers, I guess it all happened so fast, it was shocking, she thought she was going to beat it and her focus was on her son and her new husband. Of course it was. How selfish of me to think otherwise.

The most unfortunate part of this entire situation for me is, Crystal and I were extremely close when I lived in Ottawa.

We lived, loved, laughed and celebrated life a lot together. However, when I moved to Kingston, we kinda grew apart. We still chatted online and visited each other from time to time, but she is one of my special ones that I pushed aside this year. She invited me to her wedding. It happened to fall on the same day as my daughter's big dance recital so I declined. Looking back now, I could have done both that day. Yes, it would have been difficult and exhausting to rush and travel, but I could have made time. And I didn't. Instead, I told her that I promised we would spend more time together when things weren't so crazy and busy for ME.

Well, little did I know, she did not have a lot of time left. And I took that for granted.

Now don't get me wrong. I am not focusing on the "could haves", "should haves" or "would haves" and beating myself up over this. I did that for a day and then I snapped out of that thinking pretty quickly!

I learned a HUGE positive lesson from this entire situation and I know that Crystal is still smiling down on me despite my misgivings. Now, I am sharing this experience with you because I want to acknowledge how special Crystal was to me and how important it is to never take time for granted with your special ones.

Sometimes you need to slow down, take a look around and pay attention. It is an essential part of recognizing what's most important and making the most of every moment!

I hope that my special angel Crystal touches your heart and soul through this story as she has touched mine. <3

# CONCLUSION

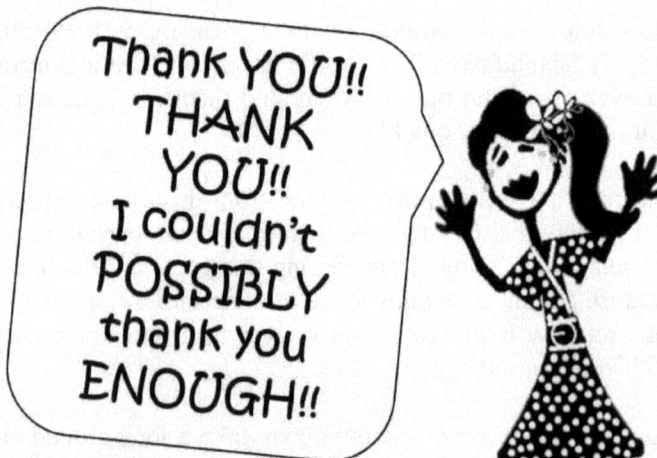

Thank YOU!!
THANK
YOU!!
I couldn't
POSSIBLY
thank you
ENOUGH!!

©2013 Comic Strip Mama Enterprises Inc.

Thank you SO MUCH for being awesome, for taking time to read this book and for laughing and sharing with me on my social media platforms. It wouldn't be possible for me to do what I love to do, if it wasn't for you supporting me throughout my journey! <3

Make sure you visit the Comic Strip Mama™ website, subscribe to the blog and sign up for AWESOME email updates!

www.comicstripmama.com

Connect with me on Facebook, Twitter and Pinterest!

www.facebook.com/ComicStripMama

www.twitter.com/ComicStripMama

www.pinterest.com/ComicStripMama

Official Comic Strip Mama™ Merchandise is now available!
Check out the shop! www.cafepress.com/comicstripmama

# About the Author

"Internet famous" for her humorous and inspirational self-syndicated webcomics about surviving the insanity of life and parenthood, Tanya Masse, AKA: "Comic Strip Mama" is a mama, a writer, a cartoonist and an entrepreneur who has faced a tremendous amount of adversity throughout the challenges of her life and has risen above it all!

Through her comics, award winning blog, social media platforms and literary works, she entertains and encourages others to:

*Make the best of the busyness, craziness, chaos, frustrations and challenges of life and parenthood!

*Live on the AWESOME side!

*STOP taking life SO SERIOUSLY!

*Embrace the INSANITY!

*Focus on the POSITIVE lessons!

*Recognize the BLESSINGS!

*Find the HUMOR whenever possible, and CELEBRATE LIFE!

www.ingramcontent.com/pod-product-compliance
Lightning Source LLC
Chambersburg PA
CBHW052005090426
42741CB00008B/1552